Contents

Contents

On the
Rob

Brandon Robshaw

Published in association with
The Basic Skills Agency

Hodder & Stoughton

A MEMBER OF THE HODDER HEADLINE GROUP

Acknowledgements
Cover: Barry Downard
Illustrations: Ben Hasler

Orders: please contact Bookpoint Ltd, 130 Milton Park, Abingdon, Oxon OX14
4SB. Telephone: (44) 01235 827720, Fax: (44) 01235 400454. Lines are open from
9.00–6.00, Monday to Saturday, with a 24 hour message answering service. You
can also order through our website: www.hodderheadline.co.uk.

British Library Cataloguing in Publication Data
A catalogue record for this title is available from The British Library

ISBN 0 340 87660 3

First published 2003
Impression number 10 9 8 7 6 5 4 3 2 1
Year   2007 2006 2005 2004 2003

Typeset by SX Composing DTP, Rayleigh, Essex.
Printed in Great Britain for Hodder & Stoughton Educational, a division of
Hodder Headline, 338 Euston Road, London NW1 3BH by Athenaeum Press,
Gateshead, Tyne and Wear.

1

'I Don't Know'

'Are you ready?' said Gemma.

'What if we get caught?' asked Liz.

'We won't get caught.
I've done it loads of times.'

The mall was crowded.
It was nearly Christmas.
A tall Christmas tree stood
in the centre of the mall.
Christmas carols were playing
over the speakers.

'Look at all these crowds,' said Gemma.
'We'll never get caught.
They'll be too busy to see us.'

'I don't know,' said Liz.
'I don't know if I like it.
It's stealing, isn't it?'

'It's not like stealing from a person.
These big shops
have got loads of money.
They can afford it, can't they?'

'I suppose so,' said Liz.
'But I'm scared.'

'Of course you're scared.
That's part of the fun!
It's part of the thrill.
Are you up for it, or not?'

'I . . . I don't know.'

Gemma looked cross.
'I thought you were my friend.
I thought you were up for a bit of fun.
But if you want to be a wimp, fine.
Run off home to Mummy,
why don't you?'

'No,' said Liz.
She didn't want Gemma to think
she was a wimp.
She wanted Gemma to be her friend.
'Well . . . OK,' she said.
'I'll do it.'

'Good!' said Gemma.
'Let's go on the rob!'

2
Make-up

Liz followed Gemma into a shop.
A security guard stood at the door.
He was a big man in uniform.
Liz felt her heart beating fast.

She following Gemma
to the make-up counter.
Gemma started picking things up –
lipsticks, eye-shadow, blusher.
She looked at each one,
then put it back.
Just as if she was deciding
what to buy.

Then she put a lipstick into her bag.
She did it very quickly and smoothly.
Liz hardly even saw her do it.
Gemma didn't look nervous at all.
She was as cool as a cucumber.
She looked at a few more things.
Then she moved slowly away.

It was Liz's turn.
She went up to the counter.
She started picking things up
and putting them back.
Luckily, the shop was crowded.
No one was looking at her.
She grabbed an eye shadow
and stuffed it into her bag.

She turned to go.
A shop assistant was standing
right in front of her.
'Can I help you?'

3
Coffee and Cream Cakes

Liz's heart beat even faster.
'No thanks – just looking,'
she said.

She walked quickly out of the shop.
She felt the security guard's eyes on her.

Then she was outside in the mall again.
Her legs felt weak and trembly.

Gemma was waiting for her.
They walked off together.
'Did you get anything?'
asked Gemma.

Liz opened her bag just a little
and showed Gemma the eye shadow.
'Not bad,' said Gemma.

Suddenly Liz began to laugh.
She didn't know why.
She couldn't stop.
Gemma started to laugh too.
They held on to each other and laughed
until they were out of breath.

'Come on,' said Gemma at last.
'Let's get something to eat.'

They went to a cafe.
They ordered coffee and cream cakes.
Liz was very pleased with herself.
She'd done it!
Without getting caught!

'What shall we do next?'
asked Gemma.
'Do you want to do another shop?'

Liz felt her heart beating fast again.
'Sure,' she said. 'Why not?'

4

The Department Store

'What about there?' asked Gemma.
She was pointing
to a large department store.
A large model of Father Christmas
stood in the window.
Reindeer were all around him.
In another window stood a Christmas tree
with presents underneath.

'Do you think it will be safe?' asked Liz.
'I mean, in these big stores
they have lots of security guards.
Cameras everywhere.'

'Don't worry,' said Gemma.
'It will be too crowded
for anyone to notice us.'

'Well . . . OK,' said Liz.

'OK! Let's go on the rob!' said Gemma.

She walked towards the door.
Liz followed her.
A blast of warm air hit them
as they went through the door.

5

The Security Guard

The store was very crowded.
No one took any notice of them.
They went to the toiletries department.
Liz saw Gemma slip a bottle of shampoo
into her bag.
Gemma moved slowly away
to another counter.
She picked up some bubble bath.
She slipped that into her bag, too.
She was very good at it, thought Liz.
So cool, so smooth, so quick.

Liz picked up a bar of soap.
She sniffed it.

It smelt of wild strawberries. Very nice.
She looked round quickly.
No one was watching.
She slipped the soap into her bag.

Gemma caught her eye and smiled.
Liz gave her a thumbs-up sign.

Suddenly,
Liz noticed a man watching them.
He didn't look like a security guard.
He didn't have a uniform.
He was wearing jeans and a black jumper.
He carried a shopping bag.
But he didn't seem
to be doing any shopping.

He was watching people.
And he had his eye on Liz and Gemma.
How long had he been watching?
Liz felt her blood run cold.

She went over to Gemma.
She caught her arm.
'That man,' she whispered.
'He's watching us.'

'Are you sure?'

'Yes! I think he's a security guard
in plain clothes.'

'Don't look so worried!' said Gemma.
'Try and act normal.
Let's make for the exit.
Nice and slow. Nice and cool.'

They walked over to the escalator.

'Is he following us?' asked Gemma.

Liz looked round quickly.
The man was at the top of the escalator.
'Yes,' she said.

6
Shoplifting

It was crowded on the ground floor.
Gemma and Liz stayed close together.
They moved through the crowd.
Liz hoped the man would lose them.

Suddenly, Liz felt a tug on her bag.
She looked round.
Her bag was hanging open.
She couldn't see who had done it.
Gemma was right next to her.

'Did you see that?' Liz asked her.
'Someone tried to steal my stuff!'

'I didn't see anything,' said Gemma
'It's terrible though.
Some people are so dishonest.'

'Where is the man?' asked Gemma.

'I can't see him.'

'Let's run for it!' said Gemma.

They broke through the crowd
and ran out into the mall.

A hand landed on Liz's shoulder.
Then on Gemma's shoulder.

It was the man in the black jumper.
A security guard was with him.

'Come back inside,' said the man.
'I have reason to believe
you've been shoplifting.'

7
The Manager

The man took them
to the top floor.
The security guard came with them.
No one spoke.
Liz felt like crying.

They went along a passage
and came to a door at the end.
'Manager,' it said,
in large gold letters.

The man tapped on the door.
'Come in!' said a voice.

The manager was a tall woman
with glasses.

'I caught these two shoplifting,'
said the man.

'I see,' said the woman.
Her voice was cold and hard.
'Empty your bags.'

Gemma opened her bag.
She took everything out.
Keys.
Mobile phone.
Make-up bag.
Purse.
Travelcard.

That was it.
No shampoo.
No bubble bath.
No stolen goods at all!

Liz stared at Gemma in surprise.
How had she got rid of it all?

'Now you,' said the manager to Liz.
With trembling hands,
Liz opened her bag.
She took out the soap she had stolen.
Then a bottle of shampoo.
Then a bottle of bubble bath.

It was all there.
Not just the stuff she'd taken.
But the stuff Gemma had taken too.

With a sick feeling,
Liz realized what had happened.
Gemma had slipped the stuff into her bag.
She'd done it in the middle of the crowd.
Just before they'd run from the shop.
That was how her bag came to be open.

Liz looked at Gemma.
Gemma did not meet her eyes.

'You can go,' the manager said to Gemma.
'But not you,' she said to Liz.
'You stay here.
I'm calling the police.'

'What will my dad say?' said Liz.

'You should have thought of that
before you started shoplifting,'
said the manager, in her cold, hard voice.

The door closed behind Gemma.
Liz burst into tears.

8
Gemma's Bag

Gemma stood at the bus stop.
It was cold and dark.
The streets were full of people
carrying bags full of Christmas shopping.
A band played Christmas carols.

What a narrow escape, thought Gemma!
It was a good job
she'd planted the stuff on Liz.
Of course, Liz would be cross about it.
That was just too bad, wasn't it?
After all, there was no point
in both of them getting caught.

The bus arrived.
The crowd at the bus stop
pushed and shoved, trying to get on.
In the crowd,
Gemma felt a sharp tug at her bag.
She tried to grab it, but too late.
The bag slipped down her arm
and then it was gone.
She managed to turn round.

A man had grabbed her bag.
He was about thirty, unshaven.

'Stop him!' shouted Gemma.
'He's got my bag!'

People turned to stare.

The man ran down the street.
He dodged in and out of the crowd.
He turned a corner
and he was gone.

Gemma's bag had gone with him.
Her keys had gone.
Her mobile phone had gone.
Her make-up bag had gone.
Her purse had gone –
and it had forty pounds in it.
Her travelcard had gone.
So she couldn't even catch the bus home.

The band started playing 'Silent Night'.

Gemma burst into tears.